Copyright © 2020 All rights reserved.

Matt D'Aquino and Beyond Grappling retains 100% rights to this material and it may not be republished, redistributed or altered in any way without the written consent of Matt D'Aquino from www.beyondgrappling.com.
NOTICE: You do not have the right to reprint, sell, give away or share the content of this book
ALL RIGHTS RESERVED.
No part of this report may be reproduced or transmitted in any form whatsoever, electronic, or mechanical, including photocopying, recording, or by any informational storage or retrieval system without express written, dated and signed permission from the author. Thanks to Murray Simons, Xavier Barker and Craig Brown for your assistance putting this book together.

ISBN: 978-0-6489653-4-3

Mamalithi ndrru'a lwamra mathamra, amra matha njenjenighinhikumu ngyunhu Jigoro Kano-ku.

JUDO
Cha Rrurimri

Lu Matt D'Aquino ndudhuthu ndrru'a mamalithinjagha
Lu Craig Brown mamalithingi picha njagha
Lu Xavier Barker ndudhuthu ndrru'a Mpakwithinjenighi

Japanngi, amra Samurai (ma-twininga puthuku) tava mbrandrra laeghae.
Amra ningi nje enam, jiujitsurru twiningafrighi.

Varaka, lu Jigoro Kano niighipwa schoolngu bullyghinhikamu. Lu pudhipwa, amra weeghe. 'ani ngyunhu chwagha: lu jujutsurru puthukunjengana.

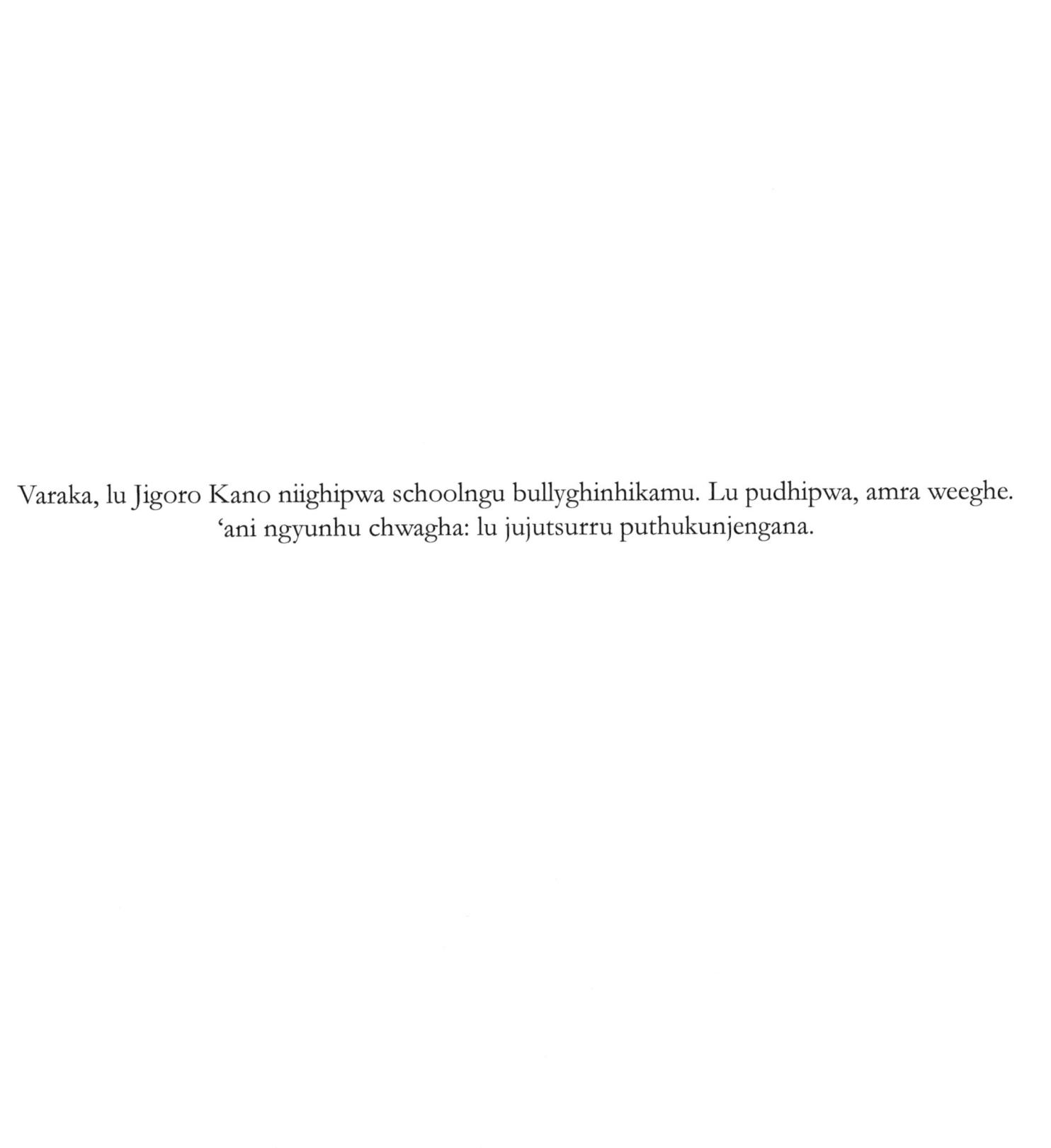

Lu Kano Sensei kanhangagha, lu punhukumu yughu tumana. Lu judo-training themechi angagha; lu ma njii'ghii, pughu.

Lu njanga judorru pughu. Lu ngyunhu ndrryamra dhayagha, lu njama maeghae.

Lu judorru kati'i njenjenighi, themechi punhukumu. Lu techniqueithi pu-pughu; technique puchiki mapwaka yupatha. Lu Kano mapwa, kayunjenginhikumu.

Lu Kano techniqueithi njenjengakunjaa. Lu Kano mathaka wa'athimri, lu techniqueiki wa'athimri. Lu Kano techniqueiki ndreeninjenighi, mapwa mbwiinhiikumu. Techniqueirri i leverageirri wambrama, ma-puthuku mbwiinii.

Lu Kano sytemnga nje kayi-kayi technique chwakagha. 1882-ngu, ngyumra Judo-school pathagha – Kodokan ngyumra nduwidhi. Ngyumra Kano twininga-art njenjenga Kano Jujutsu ngyumra nduwidhi, Kodokan Judo ngyumra nduwidhi uwkunu.

Lu Kano systemnga, lu Kano rungga-chwe-nje mbangagha. Rungga mbrandra chumu:

- Nhamra waka pudhipwa; nhamra result weeghe: mapwa ma puthuku mbwiinii, wakarra pudhipwa.

- Mbwi njenjenipri'i: kati'i ndrru njenjenini, mbwi njenjenini.

- Ndrru perfectionngi anga'a: ndrru yughu dhwimi'i, mbepenje, themechi nje pu'u.

Lu Kano lwanha Judorru chaaghaa – niighithi, lanthithi, ma weeghe, mapwa, nduprighithi, wathayi, mawkiwghithi i lamalathithi. Lu Judo pathagha, mbwi chwe puthuku punu yughu dhayanhakumu.

Lu techniqueithi nggafra nyighi, lu mbunhu njii chaaghaa. Lu mbunhu chwagha - mbwi njenjenipri'i. Lu mbunhu chwagha: Judo ngge'e sport: Judo tavarra nje ndrrandathana.

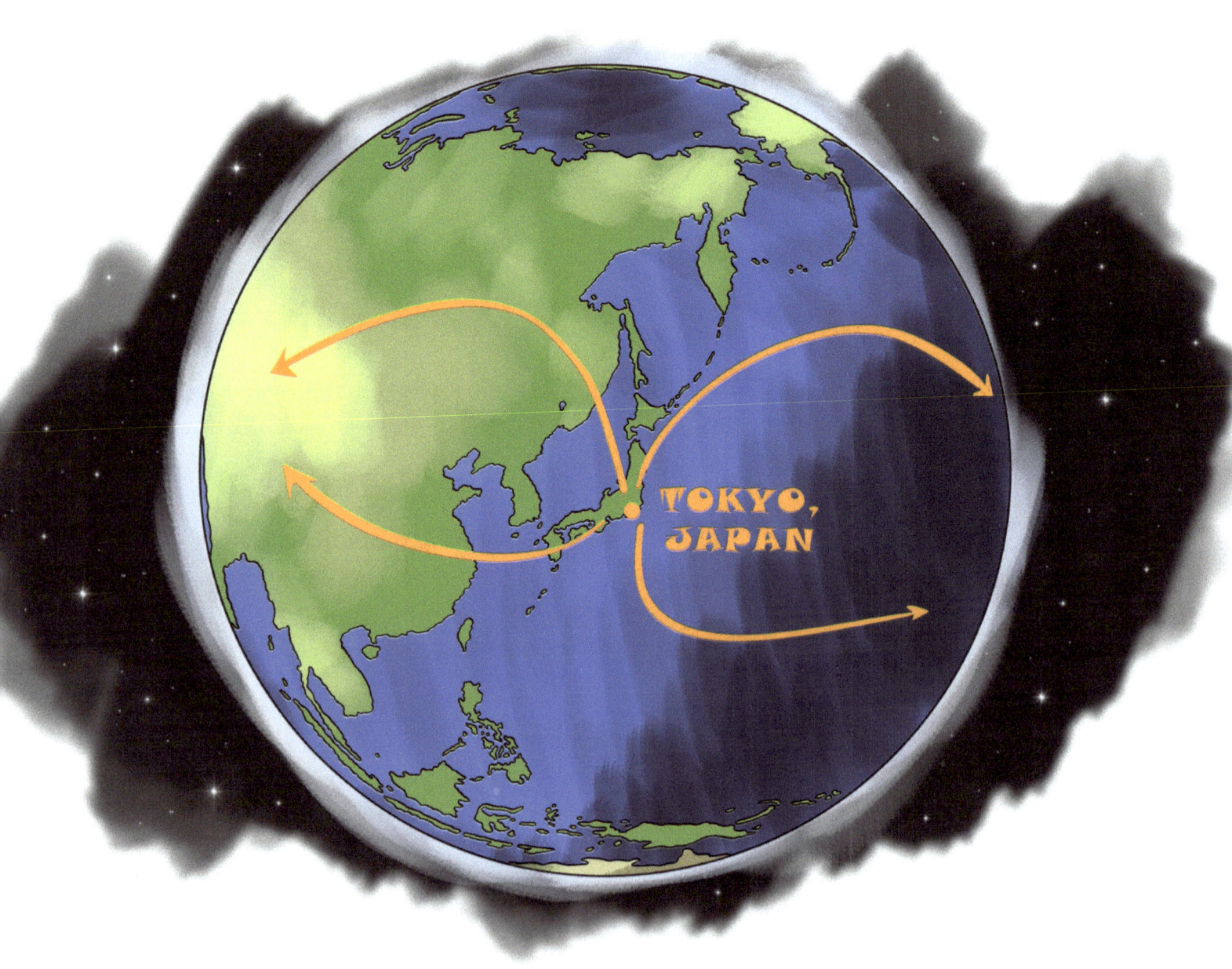

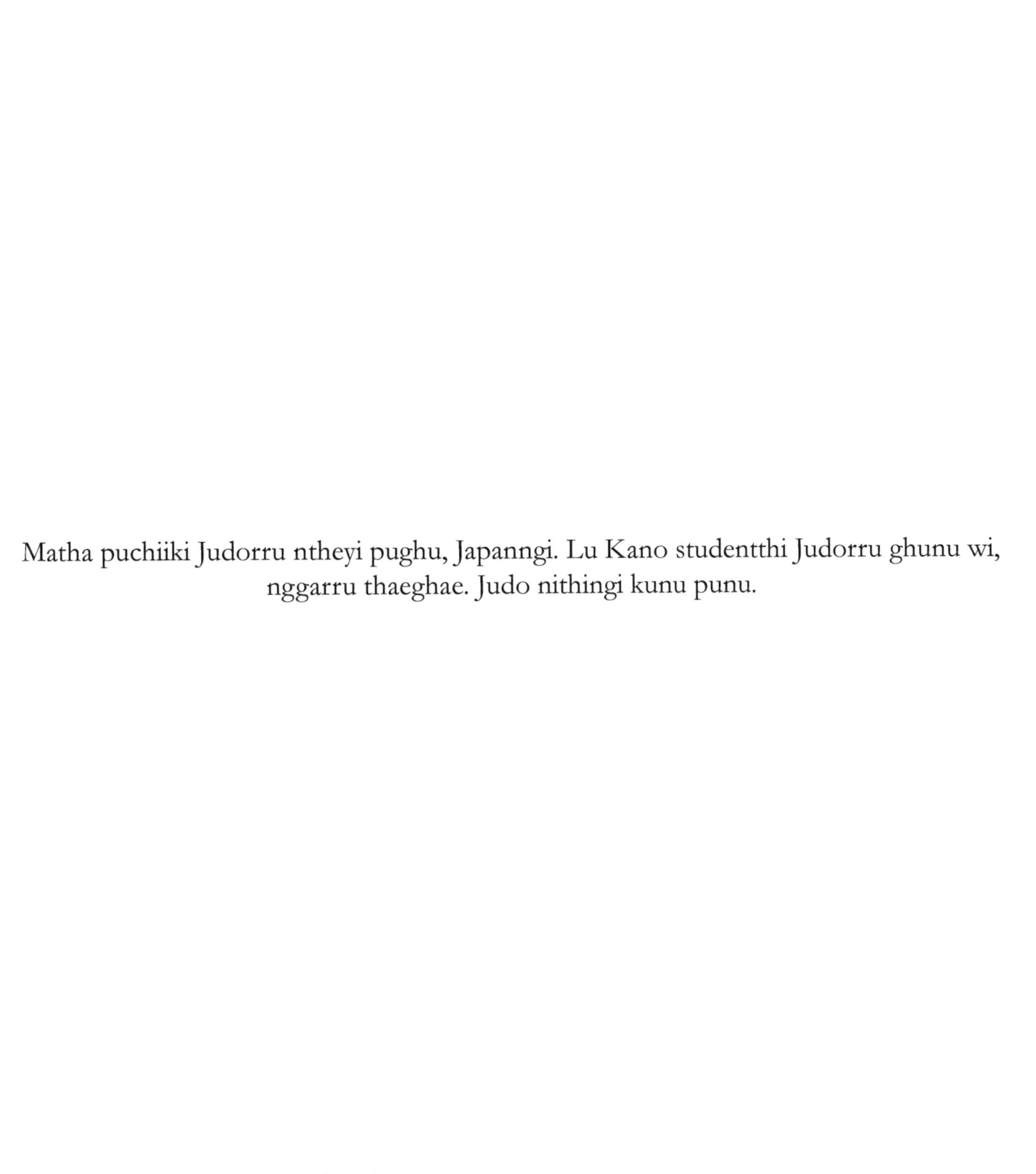

Matha puchiiki Judorru ntheyi pughu, Japanngi. Lu Kano studentthi Judorru ghunu wi, nggarru thaeghae. Judo nithingi kunu punu.

Mbwi Judongu pananjengana. Mbwi Judongu njenjengana, pay dhuwi-dhuwi-kuchana. Mbwi njenjenithini.

Ndrru njumumu twiningana, yunjumumu twiningana, kata punu, refereeing punu, coaching punu. Ndrru Judorru themechi punu, njenjenithini!

Mbwi Kanoka njenjenini, lu wa'athimri, martial art chwe nje pathagha. Lu mbu'u puthuka, yughu thaeghae: mbwi Judoka puthukunjenganhakumu.

Ndrru Judoka kunu wa'athimrinjenini. Raerrae nhanha Judonga puyu?

About the Author:

Matt D'Aquino is a Judo Olympian and author from Canberra, Australia. He has represented Australia at eight Continental Championships, four World Championships and competed in the 2008 Beijing Olympic Games. He is also a Brazilian Jiu jitsu Black Belt.

Matt is passionate about teaching and has helped thousands of grapplers worldwide through his online Judo resources, eBooks and online content which can be found at beyondgrappling.com and universityofjudo.com.

About the Illustrator:

Craig Brown is a digital media professional and freelance artist based in the Northern Territory, Australia. Craig is a judoka with over ten years of experience in Judo, currently training and coaching at Top End Judo Academy. Craig loves Judo almost as much as he loves drawing, as Judo completely changed his life for the better.

About the Translator:

Xavier Barker is a revivalistics specialist with the Pama Language Centre, based in Cape York, Australia. Xavier also coaches No Limits (Special Needs) Judo and Kata at the Cairns Judo Club.

About Mpakwithi:

Traditionally, the Mpakwithi resided on country at the junction of Tent Pole Creek and the Wenlock River, on the West Coast of Australia's Cape York Peninsula. In 1963, their homes, school, co-op store and Church was razed to the ground by Queensland police to make way for a Comalco mining lease that still hasn't been realised. The population was split between towns at Napranum, Weipa and New Mapoon.

Today, sisters Agnes Mark, Victoria Kennedy and Susan Kennedy and their cousin Celia Fletcher work with Pama Language Centre linguist Xavier Barker to revitalize their language, recruiting new speakers all the time and developing novel and innovative ways to transmit the language.

More information on the Mpakwithi can be found at www.pamacentre.org.au/mbakwithi

www.ingramcontent.com/pod-product-compliance
Lightning Source LLC
Chambersburg PA
CBHW061135010526
44107CB00068B/2951